THIS CRUISE JOURNAL
BELONGS TO:

PORT

Date:

Country: City:

MORNING EXCURSION PLANNED:

BUS TOUR: CITY HOP-ON-HOP OFF

POINTS OF INTEREST:

MUSEUMS, GALLERIES AND MONUMENTS

LUNCH
AFTERNOON EXCURSION

SHOPPING
TIME DUE BACK AT SHIP 1 HOUR BEFORE SAILAWAY

DON'T BE LATE...

THINGS WE DID AND ENJOYED IN THIS PORT

_____

_____

_____

_____

_____

SPECIAL PHOTOS

_____

_____

_____

_____

SOUVENIRS

_____

_____

_____

NOTES

NOTES

NOTES

SUNDOWNERS

DINNER

SHOW

PORT

Date:

Country: City:

MORNING EXCURSION PLANNED:

BUS TOUR: CITY HOP-ON-HOP OFF

POINTS OF INTEREST:

MUSEUMS, GALLERIES AND MONUMENTS

LUNCH
AFTERNOON EXCURSION

SHOPPING

TIME DUE BACK AT SHIP 1 HOUR BEFORE SAILAWAY

DON'T BE LATE...

THINGS WE DID AND ENJOYED IN THIS PORT

_____

_____

_____

_____

_____

_____

SPECIAL PHOTOS

_____

_____

_____

_____

_____

SOUVENIRS

_____

_____

NOTES

NOTES

NOTES

SUNDOWNERS

_____

_____

_____

_____

_____

DINNER

_____

_____

_____

_____

_____

_____

_____

_____

SHOW

_____

_____

_____

_____

_____

SEA DAY

PORT

Date:

Country: City:

MORNING EXCURSION PLANNED:

BUS TOUR: CITY HOP-ON-HOP OFF

POINTS OF INTEREST:

MUSEUMS, GALLERIES AND MONUMENTS

LUNCH

AFTERNOON EXCURSION

SHOPPING

TIME DUE BACK AT SHIP 1 HOUR BEFORE SAILAWAY

DON'T BE LATE...

THINGS WE DID AND ENJOYED IN THIS PORT

_____

_____

_____

_____

_____

_____

SPECIAL PHOTOS

_____

_____

_____

_____

SOUVENIRS

_____

_____

_____

NOTES

NOTES

NOTES

SUNDOWNERS

_____
_____
_____
_____
_____

DINNER

_____
_____
_____
_____
_____
_____
_____
_____
_____

SHOW

_____
_____
_____
_____
_____

PORT

Date:

Country: City:

MORNING EXCURSION PLANNED:

BUS TOUR: CITY HOP-ON-HOP OFF

POINTS OF INTEREST:

MUSEUMS, GALLERIES AND MONUMENTS

LUNCH
AFTERNOON EXCURSION

SHOPPING

TIME DUE BACK AT SHIP 1 HOUR BEFORE SAILAWAY

```
┌──────────────┐
│              │
└──────────────┘
```

DON'T BE LATE...

THINGS WE DID AND ENJOYED IN THIS PORT

_____

_____

_____

_____

_____

_____

SPECIAL PHOTOS

_____

_____

_____

_____

_____

SOUVENIRS

_____

_____

_____

NOTES

NOTES

NOTES

SUNDOWNERS

_____

_____

_____

_____

_____

_____

DINNER

_____

_____

_____

_____

_____

_____

_____

_____

_____

SHOW

_____

_____

_____

_____

_____

SEA DAY

_____

_____

_____

_____

_____

_____

_____

_____

_____

_____

_____

_____

_____

_____

_____

_____

_____

_____

_____

_____

_____

_____

PORT

Date:

Country: City:

MORNING EXCURSION PLANNED:

BUS TOUR: CITY HOP-ON-HOP OFF

POINTS OF INTEREST:

MUSEUMS, GALLERIES AND MONUMENTS

LUNCH

AFTERNOON EXCURSION

SHOPPING

TIME DUE BACK AT SHIP 1 HOUR BEFORE SAILAWAY

DON'T BE LATE...

THINGS WE DID AND ENJOYED IN THIS PORT

_____

_____

_____

_____

_____

SPECIAL PHOTOS

_____

_____

_____

_____

SOUVENIRS

_____

_____

NOTES

NOTES

NOTES

SUNDOWNERS

_____

_____

_____

_____

_____

_____

DINNER

_____

_____

_____

_____

_____

_____

_____

_____

_____

SHOW

_____

_____

_____

_____

_____

PORT

Date:

Country: City:

MORNING EXCURSION PLANNED:

BUS TOUR: CITY HOP-ON-HOP OFF

POINTS OF INTEREST:

MUSEUMS, GALLERIES AND MONUMENTS

LUNCH
AFTERNOON EXCURSION

SHOPPING
TIME DUE BACK AT SHIP 1 HOUR BEFORE SAILAWAY

☐

DON'T BE LATE...

THINGS WE DID AND ENJOYED IN THIS PORT

_____

_____

_____

_____

_____

SPECIAL PHOTOS

_____

_____

_____

_____

SOUVENIRS

_____

_____

_____

NOTES

NOTES

NOTES

SUNDOWNERS

_____
_____
_____
_____

DINNER

_____
_____
_____
_____
_____
_____
_____
_____

SHOW

_____
_____
_____
_____
_____

SEA DAY

PORT

Date:

Country: City:

MORNING EXCURSION PLANNED:

BUS TOUR: CITY HOP-ON-HOP OFF

POINTS OF INTEREST:

MUSEUMS, GALLERIES AND MONUMENTS

LUNCH
AFTERNOON EXCURSION

SHOPPING
TIME DUE BACK AT SHIP 1 HOUR BEFORE SAILAWAY

```
┌──────────────┐
│              │
└──────────────┘
```

DON'T BE LATE...

THINGS WE DID AND ENJOYED IN THIS PORT

_____

_____

_____

_____

_____

_____

SPECIAL PHOTOS

_____

_____

_____

_____

_____

SOUVENIRS

_____

_____

_____

NOTES

NOTES

NOTES

SUNDOWNERS

DINNER

SHOW

PORT

Date:

Country: City:

MORNING EXCURSION PLANNED:

BUS TOUR: CITY HOP-ON-HOP OFF

POINTS OF INTEREST:

MUSEUMS, GALLERIES AND MONUMENTS

LUNCH
AFTERNOON EXCURSION

SHOPPING
TIME DUE BACK AT SHIP 1 HOUR BEFORE SAILAWAY

DON'T BE LATE...

THINGS WE DID AND ENJOYED IN THIS PORT

_____

_____

_____

_____

_____

_____

SPECIAL PHOTOS

_____

_____

_____

_____

SOUVENIRS

_____

_____

_____

NOTES

NOTES

NOTES

_____

_____

_____

_____

_____

_____

_____

_____

_____

_____

_____

_____

_____

_____

_____

_____

_____

_____

_____

_____

_____

SUNDOWNERS

DINNER

SHOW

SEA DAY

_____

_____

_____

_____

_____

_____

_____

_____

_____

_____

_____

_____

_____

_____

_____

_____

_____

_____

_____

_____

_____

_____

PORT

Date:

Country: City:

MORNING EXCURSION PLANNED:

BUS TOUR: CITY HOP-ON-HOP OFF

POINTS OF INTEREST:

MUSEUMS, GALLERIES AND MONUMENTS

LUNCH

AFTERNOON EXCURSION

SHOPPING

TIME DUE BACK AT SHIP 1 HOUR BEFORE SAILAWAY

DON'T BE LATE...

THINGS WE DID AND ENJOYED IN THIS PORT

_____

_____

_____

_____

_____

SPECIAL PHOTOS

_____

_____

_____

_____

SOUVENIRS

_____

_____

_____

NOTES

NOTES

NOTES

SUNDOWNERS

_____
_____
_____
_____
_____

DINNER

_____
_____
_____
_____
_____
_____
_____
_____
_____

SHOW

_____
_____
_____
_____
_____

PORT

Date:

Country: City:

___

MORNING EXCURSION PLANNED:

___

___

___

BUS TOUR: CITY HOP-ON-HOP OFF

___

___

___

POINTS OF INTEREST:

___

___

___

MUSEUMS, GALLERIES AND MONUMENTS

___

___

___

LUNCH
AFTERNOON EXCURSION

___

___

SHOPPING
TIME DUE BACK AT SHIP 1 HOUR BEFORE SAILAWAY

DON'T BE LATE...

THINGS WE DID AND ENJOYED IN THIS PORT

_____
_____
_____
_____
_____

SPECIAL PHOTOS

_____
_____
_____
_____

SOUVENIRS

_____
_____
_____

NOTES

NOTES

NOTES

SUNDOWNERS

_____

_____

_____

_____

_____

DINNER

_____

_____

_____

_____

_____

_____

_____

_____

SHOW

_____

_____

_____

_____

PORT

Date:

Country: City:

_____

MORNING EXCURSION PLANNED:
_____
_____

BUS TOUR: CITY HOP-ON-HOP OFF
_____
_____

POINTS OF INTEREST:
_____
_____

MUSEUMS, GALLERIES AND MONUMENTS
_____
_____

LUNCH
AFTERNOON EXCURSION
_____
_____

SHOPPING
TIME DUE BACK AT SHIP 1 HOUR BEFORE SAILAWAY

```
┌─────────────────────┐
│                     │
│                     │
└─────────────────────┘
```

DON'T BE LATE...

THINGS WE DID AND ENJOYED IN THIS PORT

_____

_____

_____

_____

_____

SPECIAL PHOTOS

_____

_____

_____

_____

SOUVENIRS

_____

_____

_____

NOTES

NOTES

NOTES

SUNDOWNERS

_____

_____

_____

_____

_____

DINNER

_____

_____

_____

_____

_____

_____

_____

_____

SHOW

_____

_____

_____

_____

_____

PORT

Date:

Country: City:

_____

MORNING EXCURSION PLANNED:

_____

_____

_____

BUS TOUR: CITY HOP-ON-HOP OFF

_____

_____

_____

POINTS OF INTEREST:

_____

_____

_____

MUSEUMS, GALLERIES AND MONUMENTS

_____

_____

_____

LUNCH
AFTERNOON EXCURSION

_____

_____

_____

SHOPPING
TIME DUE BACK AT SHIP 1 HOUR BEFORE SAILAWAY

[   ]

DON'T BE LATE...

THINGS WE DID AND ENJOYED IN THIS PORT

_____

_____

_____

_____

_____

SPECIAL PHOTOS

_____

_____

_____

SOUVENIRS

_____

_____

NOTES

NOTES

NOTES

SUNDOWNERS

_____

_____

_____

_____

_____

DINNER

_____

_____

_____

_____

_____

_____

_____

_____

_____

SHOW

_____

_____

_____

_____

_____

PORT

Date:

Country: City:

_____

MORNING EXCURSION PLANNED:

_____

_____

_____

BUS TOUR: CITY HOP-ON-HOP OFF

_____

_____

_____

POINTS OF INTEREST:

_____

_____

_____

MUSEUMS, GALLERIES AND MONUMENTS

_____

_____

_____

LUNCH

AFTERNOON EXCURSION

_____

_____

_____

SHOPPING

TIME DUE BACK AT SHIP 1 HOUR BEFORE SAILAWAY

[   ]

DON'T BE LATE...

THINGS WE DID AND ENJOYED IN THIS PORT

_____

_____

_____

_____

_____

_____

SPECIAL PHOTOS

_____

_____

_____

_____

_____

SOUVENIRS

_____

_____

_____

NOTES

NOTES

NOTES

SUNDOWNERS

_____

_____

_____

_____

_____

DINNER

_____

_____

_____

_____

_____

_____

_____

_____

_____

SHOW

_____

_____

_____

_____

_____

PORT

Date:

Country: City:

_____

MORNING EXCURSION PLANNED:

_____

_____

BUS TOUR: CITY HOP-ON-HOP OFF

_____

_____

POINTS OF INTEREST:

_____

_____

MUSEUMS, GALLERIES AND MONUMENTS

_____

_____

LUNCH
AFTERNOON EXCURSION

_____

_____

SHOPPING
TIME DUE BACK AT SHIP 1 HOUR BEFORE SAILAWAY

[   ]

DON'T BE LATE...

THINGS WE DID AND ENJOYED IN THIS PORT

_____

_____

_____

_____

_____

SPECIAL PHOTOS

_____

_____

_____

_____

SOUVENIRS

_____

_____

_____

NOTES

NOTES

NOTES

SUNDOWNERS

_____
_____
_____
_____
_____

DINNER

_____
_____
_____
_____
_____
_____
_____
_____
_____

SHOW

_____
_____
_____
_____

PORT

Date:

Country: City:

MORNING EXCURSION PLANNED:

BUS TOUR: CITY HOP-ON-HOP OFF

POINTS OF INTEREST:

MUSEUMS, GALLERIES AND MONUMENTS

LUNCH
AFTERNOON EXCURSION

SHOPPING
TIME DUE BACK AT SHIP 1 HOUR BEFORE SAILAWAY

```
┌─────────────────────┐
│                     │
└─────────────────────┘
```

DON'T BE LATE...

THINGS WE DID AND ENJOYED IN THIS PORT

_____

_____

_____

_____

_____

_____

SPECIAL PHOTOS

_____

_____

_____

_____

_____

SOUVENIRS

_____

_____

_____

NOTES

NOTES

NOTES

SUNDOWNERS

_____

_____

_____

_____

_____

DINNER

_____

_____

_____

_____

_____

_____

_____

_____

SHOW

_____

_____

_____

_____

_____

NOTES

NOTES

NOTES

NOTES

NOTES

NOTES